YOUR FUNNY, FUNNY FACE

by

Patricia Barone

BLUE LIGHT PRESS ◆ 1ST WORLD PUBLISHING

1ST WORLD
PUBLISHING

SAN FRANCISCO ◆ FAIRFIELD ◆ DELHI

1ST WORLD LIBRARY
PO Box 2211
Fairfield, IA 52556
www.1stworldpublishing.com

BLUE LIGHT PRESS
www.bluelightpress.com
bluelightpress@aol.com

BOOK & COVER ART & DESIGN
Melanie Gendron
melaniegendron999@gmail.com

COVER PHOTO
Matthew Barone

AUTHOR PHOTO
Claire Barone

photo of seafood feast, unknown, Gottschalk family archive

FIRST EDITION

Library of Congress Control Number: 2018954145

ISBN 9781421838144

Acknowledgements

"I Love Your Funny, Funny Face," published as "Love Poem," in *Streamlines*, and most recently, in *Green Blade*

"Fishing," in *Going to the Lake*, Loonfeather Press

"On the Primal Embarrassment of Mothers," *Revival* (Limerick, Ireland)

"A First Weaving," *Green Blade*

"My Shadows, Our Light," *Green Blade*

"Grace," also appeared in *The Scent of Water*, Patricia Barone, Blue Light Press

"Frozen Lake" and "Your Eyes Possessed," Wising Up Press

Your Funny, Funny Face

A Collection of Poetry

In memory of my husband, Stan T. Barone

and dedicated to his beloved sister,
my dear friend, Maizie Ray.

As always, these poems are for Matt and Claire.

Table of Contents

Entering Your Face

Lake Pontchartrain Feast

Gulping the lake, he chokes.
Nuncio hauls him up by his trunks
and pushes his stomach till he burps
brackish water. Uck! Like raw catfish.

Stan flops along the sea wall. "Don't cry!"
his dad says, "you swallowed a fish 'n' spit it up —
Look!" A wriggling minnow in his big hand.
"Too small, we hafta throw 'er back!"
High glinting in the sun, then a tiny splash.

The uncles are dragging up the metal traps,
full of maroon mudbugs — his dad helps Stan
pull one cage in, the crawfish crawling
under and over each other.
Nuncio tells Stan how to hold blue crabs
behind the big pincer claws —
Or it's "Snip, snip — no fingers."

Back on Bayou St. John, Ethel, Stan's mother,
spreads newspaper on long trestle tables,
as Nuncio dumps the seafood in the boiling kettle.
Splash! Hot salty drops blister Stan's arm.

He runs off to play with his sister Maizie
and seven cousins. Jostling, sweaty,
they compete for seats at the table and brag
about who has the highest stack of empty shells.

Mom and Dad, aunts and uncles, eat forever.
Stan and the other kids play Cowboys and Indians
on the crushed shell driveway and vacant lot,

where Uncle Chester boarded his cow for the war.
Mom milked it, and Stan gave it straw to eat.
Beneath an apple tree, good ol' dog Spanky sleeps.

After bagging the shells, they eat chocolate macaroons,
pralines, and bread pudding with that rum sauce
that makes you want to lick the bowl and get drunk.
The grownups get sillier. Stan's own mother
wears a gardenia behind her ear and his dad has beers.
Then iced coffee, and all the kids get root beer floats
but Aunt Nellie's cry baby, who has milk.

A poinsettia tall as the roof makes a shady place
to watch the sun go down in time for fireworks.
Through Stan's closing lids, he sees a red cloud
in a white sky—a giant red crab and a swordfish
swimming under him. So he grabbed its fins.
"Don't swim out too far," his mother warns the fish.
Boom! And his dad reaches down to haul him up
to fireflies, rockets, and exploding pink magnolias.

On the Primal Embarrassment of Mothers

There she was, my mother — she spit
on the sidewalk. She didn't care.
I crossed the street, and tried to fit
my steps to cracks in the cement,
breaking her back — she was so sure,
so comfortable, my mother — she spit
anywhere she wanted. My face felt
scalded. Chin up, I watched my posture,
as I crossed the street, and tried to fit
into my uniform vest, my tight
skirt, my skin, my life. My measure
in public was my mother, who spit,
laughed loudly, farted from beer, went
out with her unshaven legs, her loose derriere.

I crossed the street away from her and tried
to fit my feet to a looser step. I'd split
home, school, the prom, and land in my future
if I could be like my mother, who spit
if I crossed the street, if I tried to fit.

Her Soul

Which was small, round and white,
was hidden in the center of her stomach.

Her dad said, "brat!"
She'd never looked
inside the mirror to see if she
or someone bad peeked out her eyes.

Was her real self crouched inside,
arms hugging knees?
Would she be too ashamed to lift her head?

She peered into her own mirror eyes,
hazel like tea on top,
dark below as Mrs. Olson's well.

Seeing a small self in her pupils
looking sad, she knew
she was only wounded.

She spoke to her soul —
"Get stronger!"

That Creased Map

Chewing Juicy Fruit and wearing shiny Mary Janes,
I jumped onboard the train — Chicago with my Dad!
The porter let me feed the birds, and then —
clickety clack — the wheels squashed crumbs.
Behind us, tracks of rails, the snow crusts black.

We saw Burton Holmes, the great explorer,
his slides of Africa, his pointer in the Sahara,
and me, only nine, sitting in a velvet seat
next to my father, who called me Queen.
At home he worked too hard for us,
and I was an awful bother.

In the diner, my hot cocoa raced
around its rim, shaky but not spilling,
like me when I've talked back to Dad.
The morning after I cried myself to sleep
I woke up somewhere else on that creased map.

The Bride and Groom

Three hours before the wedding, the bride
is still sewing pearls on her white Juliette cap,
smiling though terrified. Her dad prescribes half
a tranquilizer with 7-Up.

At two hours to go, one red velvet
bridesmaid neckline left to bead.
No lies about wearing it again.
"Let your sister sew it herself!"
Her mother makes her take a hot bath.

The poor groom who, at the stag party,
left the toboggan head first, losing his hat
to the tree he hit! His wedding headache
was not because of whiskey but her wild
Irish cousin, the one who'd steered.

She disembarks from the car at the church
but slips and slides on ice. The groom skids
to her side; they twist and turn but don't fall.
The bride looks into the groom's brown eyes,
bright with tears of laughter.

She clutches his hands.
When the church dims and candle flames leap,
and even relatives, friends, and celebrant subside,
they breathe, feel calm seeing each other.
She'll say anything, her lips no longer trembling,
if he will say it too. And so they do.

Our Backward Forward Dream

We're also married to our privacies.
In sleep, we print old pictures,
fuse our dreams, making our double exposure —
A circle-dissolve and we watch you
put a penny on the frosted pane.

The children skating past dark
on the pond are you and me.
No one tends the wood stove,
as we take off our skates in the cold.

In bed your feet are icy on my ankles.
You wake me in the middle of another
dream of aching repetition,
fragments of night.

You're small, and it rains in your big boots.
You hide the note from Miss Brust —
You didn't do it!

Your mother, waiting with a list,
won't let you dry —
she sends you out for cigarettes.

A bull terrier nips your feet.
You cry and run for your life —
no one else will fight for you, but me.

Wake up, feel our baby.
His blind head pushes my abdomen.
We're traveling a long way to hold him.

Portrait of the Son

in memory of Ethel Barone

In her front room,
where drapes are always drawn,
she keeps his shrine.
Stan at 28, moustache like a bandito.
I painted him naked to the shoulders
and gave him to his mother.

Our children ask why their father's
eyes are red, not brown.
"It must have been cheap paint," I say.
"You never got his eyes," says Ethel.
I *did* get his hair — curly from my fingers.

She points to the velvet toreador
who faces the portrait, and says,
"Patty thinks this picture is bad art.
I love it! My young Stan
brought it back from Mexico."

"*I*, not Pat, think the picture is bad,"
Stan says and whispers I owe him one.
The bullfighter's neon, nappy cape
traps her son's foreign travel
and makes it hers.

Ethel thinks I owe him everything.
She wants him to sit with her
under the merliton vine, she wants
to give him cup after cup
of milky chicory coffee.

"It's just terrible, Stan,
Cubans gather and gesture.
They speak in their own language."
She wants to complain about me —
how outspoken I am, but he
defends me —"I love my wife!"

Meantime I go past the ice house
on the corner of his childhood,
where he ran so scared from the Ice Man,
to Salcedo Street, his grandma's house.
Pigulasto pastries rose in her oven just for him.

When I call him to come and get me,
he sits beneath the pecan tree,
and will not come to the phone
but sends our son:
"I'm Dad's special messenger."

That night our son wets his bed.
Stan rubs the stain with after shave.
He won't tell his mother till we leave.
Together, they turn the mattress over.

The Entertainer

for Stan

A double knock and "Speak of the devil."
Uncle Henry sets his pork pie hat at a jaunty angle.
"Ethel, I was telling my buddies how swell
little Stan can tap dance—I want to show 'em."

Ethel, Stan's mother, narrowed her eyes.
"No dives, Henry, nothing Scaramouche,
Deacon Jones, or Tobacco Road!
Above all not Storyville
or any other red light district!"

§

"We're right next to Storyville, Uncle Henry!"
— "Fulfilling the letter of the law, my boy!"
Stan's ears were red even before
he met his uncles' goofy friends
down at Lafitte's Blacksmith Shop
and they formed a circle for his
rapid series of shuffles, ball heels,
brushes, paradiddles and double time steps.

His arms were pumping, cheeks flushed,
and he wiped the sweat out of his eyes.
Uncle Jiggs bought him coca cola —
three swigs and Stan was back.
Coins rattled into Henry's hat.

Stan did heel-toes, his arms wind milling
for applause, then he tapped buffalos,
flat ball changes, and he bomber-shayed

to their table, up-ending his coke, glug, glug.
They bought him another and crab cakes
'n catsup-smothered fries.
"You won big for me! said Henry.
Let's go get us new tourists!"

At The Carousel, Stan did cramp rolls
and hop scuffle steps, as far as he'd gone in class.
Henry grinned. "Next week, I'll have you sing!"

Uh oh. He hopes his mom won't let him.
Something makes him feel bad
about getting down on one knee,
black shoe polish on his face,
arms outstretched singing
Mammy like Al Jolson.

His daddy used the N word
but Mom said it wasn't "refined."
She wasn't as mad as Dad
about Stan tossing the Whites-Only sign
out of the street car window.

Lucky Love

In an Orleans Parish monsoon,
the chair presided over the boulevard
as if in a formal parlor.
Pale yellow upholstery soaked,
its maple legs were tickled
by tough zoysia grass.

Stan lifted some rich someone's
discarded chair into our car, a lowly Bug.
Its wickerwork was latticed and pristine,
despite the needling rain.
We rolled up the windows, sheltering
a chair we couldn't afford.
Our life was lucky that way.

When Stan yelled, "freeze!",
I didn't step down — a water moccasin!
Curved like a cypress branch, away
it slithered in the Honey Island swamp.
More than lucky,
he was looking out for me —
the shimmering danger
of our life together.

In One Glance Alive

My husband was new to snow,
so I warned him
of hypnotic fat flakes
the soporific creak
and sweep-sweep
of wind shield wipers.

We sang to stay alert
as the blizzard buffeted
our car from side to side,
headlights reappearing
like will o' the wisps
in our white swamp.

We followed the slow snake
of highway lights for hours
until all lights melted away on glass.
We tracked red brake lights
off the ramp to Portage,
and a 2-ton truck slid
straight at us.

In the blinding glare of headlights,
Stan turned our skidding car
away from the slush-spewing truck.
The seconds we looked at each other
seemed as long as the lives we almost lost.

Harvest

I walked the echoing rooms.
Not even dust remained,
but still my soul clung
to shreds of country dreams
as I looked in every corner.

From the bloom of frost,
its flowers, stems and leaves,
etched on the window pane,
to the shuddering rattle
of the radiator hissing steam —
our small frame house
shivered as we shut the door forever
on our first years as a couple,
dark-haired strangers from big cities
in an ingrown Nordic town.

You and I, love, got what we came for —
a living from unruly students and a degree —
and more: I remember a ring of ice crystals
around the moon and my students
helping me harvest tomatoes, the ones
their father gave me as seedlings.

Housewife Blues in a Northern Winter

1. Need

Your daughter or husband, your son
eats lax of jaw.
You want to scream, Stop!
That moist animal sound.

Someone else's need
satisfied.
Yours in you still.

2. Habit

For a week it just lies there
among shrunken tomatoes
on the bamboo mat. From a can
of mixed vegetables, like
a consumer prize —
this bone.

Every day I look at it,
A finger bone, I'm thinking, as I cut
the roast, my hands assured. Knuckles
have cauliflower knobs.

Of the many things to speak of,
should I venture, "There's this bone
showing marrow at the joint."

"It's a twig," he'll say and I'll reply,
"Whose bone is this?" or
"Why do we do what we do?"

Housewife Blues in a Northern Winter

3. The Cage

The male parakeet,
acid green hood, red beak,
pecks the feathers off
the neck of his setting female.

What is it about
this ordinary cage,
each bar as thin and jointed as
a finger bone?

Grace

The fires we built that winter
were feeble and scanned
the newspapers in one scorch,
leaving each sheet whole but charred.
Black words dropped into the cinders.

Pine kept its cold green heart,
bark gnawed by useless matches.
Both miserly and poor,
we wore our overcoats indoors.
You rolled string. I grudged
the mice each crumb.

Late March we laid a pyre,
hard new oak on balsam.
The log drizzled sap, cracked sparks,
and blazed, as smoke possessed our room —
we'd forgotten to open the damper.

After dousing our fiasco with weak tea,
we turned our backs on the soggy grate
and waited for the hearth to dry.

We could have scraped the bricks
or gathered sticks, but we were weary,
being in a constant shiver, feeling mean.

Yellow flickering stirred the embers,
and we bent to warm our hands
on one kindling coal.

The Oldest Bed

St. Augustine, Florida
for Stan

We two could fit beneath
narrow 16th century bedding,
goose down over a horse hair pallet.
We're good campers,
compatible runts of any century,
when we're spooned together, you and I.

"Let's test the bed," you say,
making eyes at me. Sex may be funny
but love is pertinacious.
Passionflowers cling fast to walls.

Which is most sensual, I ask—
this bed, strawberries in a bowl
of clotted cream? Or Zinfandel
at the inn, that modern bed?

Lagniappe

for Stan

Almonds, my breakfast,
rest in their oval brown casings —
satisfaction without flash.

Eaten one by one,
they are never too rich,
unlike cashews,
which sate the tongue
with sweet oil.
You love
these perfectly turned horns.

You, to my tongue,
taste more like an almond,
a subtle flavor of vanilla.

You are *lagniappe*[1],
my unearned delight.

[1]a bonus, extra; an unexpected gift; in New Orleans,
pronounced "lan-y-ap" or "lan-yap."

I Love Your Funny, Funny Face

as you crouch in the back seat
with your wax false teeth
jaunting out your upper lip
so speeding cars will jerk,
heads whipping round.

One truck gunned backward,
skidding the yellow line off the road
to see you again. By then you were not
over-biting, but primly you stared,
just the swipe of a smirk.

You were pleased to suppose
some little girl would
make up a story —
how Wolf Man Jack
pulled up his fangs.

2.
Hoodiboodiba, and *cha cha cha* —
your nonsense gift of tongues for children.
Our toddler imitates your cadence,
as you cake-walk, rock and roll
till the needle jumps.
We need the street
for our Jackson-5 strut,
Elysian Fields, Mardi Gras stepping.

You mock your middle-aged gut,
balloon it under your chest,
whoosh it down with a slap on your belt.
Matt laughs, and you bend your knees,
whisk knuckles on the floor as his gorilla.

3.
Your father rolled his eyes
and bared his teeth.
My dad never meant to be absurd.
"Life is a serious business," he'd say.
"We start dying when we're born."

Since our marriage,
I've lost the dark family
circles beneath my eyes.
A missing abscessed tooth
gives my face a goofy gape.
I don't replace it.
It's part of loving you
to want a funny face.

Marriage Conversation

Marriage Conversation

*Our notion of symmetry is derived from
the human face.*
— Blaise Pascal

1.

Once we read about twins
who spoke together out of sync,
one voice after another —
lines around a jarred tracing.

Often we moved apart
into the supper chores,
still talking from a distance.
I thought I heard you say,
"Those twins are like crazed words
that attack for no reason."

I never thought words would turn on me:
"Togetherness," a cheesy out-of-date
idea from *Ladies' Home Journal.*

2.

"We are different,"
I accuse you.

How civil I could be
to someone with my faults.
how tolerant of virtue
in a stranger.

3.

"We can never know," I said,
coming up behind you at the sink,
"what we really look like
unless we have a twin."

"That's stupid, most people
have mirrors," you said.

"Ah ha! that's where you're wrong,"
said I, "We're backward in mirrors."

"There's always T.V.," you say.
"Identical twins see video.

You were a little mad because
I was talking all around the real subject —

How I wanted you to be like me,
so I'd feel comfortable married,
maybe not notice it at all.

But I didn't want marriage video.
Like a shopper caught by store TV
I was shy of my own face.

4.

You laughed at my mirror face —
And a good thing too.

Married people get too skilled at throwing
their partner's altered image back —
visual ventriloquists.

Old partners growing
to look more alike each year.
Not just that she grows chin hair,
or he develops breasts —

It's more like a blurring of their edges,
starting with their voices
in a two part harmony.

5.

Do Siamese twins take care
not to strain the skin between them?
Are they seldom graceless or forgetful?

We who live in separate bodies
suffer enough. Imagine
the looping trajectory of double pain.

6.

We're disconnected
on the telephone.

At best, you sound embarrassed,
dwindled on the line,
getting fainter like an older
printout in dot matrix.

You say I have a sensual fallacy:
"If you sat on your hands,
you couldn't say a word."

"The body doesn't lie," I say.
A disembodied voice can be

an unsuccessful foreign film.
We listen to a face
with a badly fitting voice
and believe in neither
the face nor the voice

until we put them together
from old griefs.
Mine — "I could never disagree
with my father, without crying."
Yours — "My mother wouldn't let me talk.
She slapped my face."

8.

Those Victorian family portraits:
Remember how the woman always stood
Behind her husband, hand upon his shoulder.
In their engagement photo, Grandma sits,
Her plush chair sprouting six-point antlers.
Grandpa stands behind her and he grins.
"Good for you!" I want to tell them, wishing
she looked less apprehensive.

9.

The women in my family say the most
when they're most afraid to say it.

In wordless conversation on a bridge,
we were fishing in the sun, drinking beer.

You didn't give permission to be lazy,
but your dare. Like the boy next door.

You taught me to skip pebbles,
and laughed at water rings

I projected with my voice,
not someone else's stone.

10.

Married over fifty years, my parents
never lived together long enough
to complete each other's sentences.
I wonder what is meant by a sentence?

Mom sits up at 2 a.m., worrying over her beads.
"I've changed, living with your father."
Dad insisted he never used to
"foam off at the mouth," but admits,
"I caught your mother's loose talk."

11.

A sentence begins and ends,
is a time, and like next month —
another country.

The worst part of a stroke —
one side of the mouth
drags down as if the face
mocks itself.

His wife says she knows:
"He's trying to tell me something."

She'd say it for him
if she only could.

12.

Twins don't use conversation, but ESP.
If you knew what I would say before I said it,
what need would we have for separate skin
or Plato's androgynous dream:
not the double, but the missing half.

After we make love, our joke:
"Why don't we stay this way?"
If you remained inside me,
and never had to enter,
what then?"

13.

In my dream you were
a surprise. Why else did I
sit facing you, our knees touching
as I lean to hold your face and only take
my hands away to put them back upon
your mouth, you speaking,
not separate words,
the murmur of our marriage.

Warm Braille to my fingers,
        your breath.
If I couldn't hear you
I could read your lips
and enter you, your face.

Between Weft and Warp

The Alien

1.

Six year olds talk teeth.
"I can wiggle it with my tongue."
But soon he was crying, "it hurts!"
"That's normal," I insisted;
necessary loss blinded me
to his uncommon ache.

All week I thought how appealing —
the curve of his upper lip
and missed the abscess lifting it.
His profile was too familiar.
Infection's exaggeration
helped me see his face again.

I hadn't stopped enough
to love the upward tilt of each brown eye,
the way his ears hugged his head,
though I was always there to clean them.

"There are jobs to be done
despite our aches and pains.
The older I get, the more
my knees lock," grumbled Grandpa,
who told Matt to be tough.
"Nothing worse than a whiny child."
Do other kids — the quiet kind —
drop their teeth like seeds?

I had words for Matthew, too.
"You think you have trouble?!"

He was too young to realize
how I'd crossed my bridge
and earned my three gold crowns.

2.

Now gap toothed, Matt's mouth
looks like the Martian head he made
in ceramics the day after
a dentist packed his gums with gauze.

I asked why the head's sharp teeth
were few and spread so far.
He said, "The Martian lost them
before his big teeth came —
that's why he looks so scared."

Matt gave his sculpture four ears.
The antennas resemble tongues,
but there's none in the mouth —
how hard it is for humans to explain.

Our bodies show our feelings,
molding the faces no one lets us make.
Out of the kiln, our doubles
give us back our losses.

Discovering the alien
has ordinary eyes,
we leave our sweaty fingerprints in clay.

Everything Happens Still

for Matthew at almost two

1.

The baby has your mobile now.
She waves her arms. You watch
the wooden zoo go round above her head
playing your lullaby by Brahms.

Later, when I'm changing you,
I sing your melody. You cry.
I stop — you beg for more,
"Sing lullaby," you tell me.

You cry louder than the baby,
squeezing your tears into one
mother, two or three — all yours.

2.

Till the baby came we kept
your small-child time, easy.
A turtle tracks our lawn —
we watched its wake in grass
for one whole day.
Then we blinked,
and it was gone
beneath the fence.

3.

You are gentle and don't rest
your weight upon the baby
when you kiss her. "Good boy!"
Then you push her.

I leave you in your room.
"The baby comes with me
so you can't hurt her."

You don't get your mother
back, till you're afraid
and like us all —
bewildered by your own hands
contriving to lose what you most want.

Freedom

There's no photo of me at three
crouching in the hollyhocks
with my wet pants down.
Sun is warm
on red and yellow petals
blue sky in between.
No one could have told me
doing wrong makes
everything brighter
and farther away —
like a mother.

A First Weaving

Claire's small fingers push down
a row of yellow with her comb.
She hides her face in the yarn bag
and my mother, quick, pulls
the last thread taut, smoothing
Claire's sticky knots.
Claire catches her at it.
— "I'll do it myself! Myself!"

 And Grandma bristles.
— "I only want to help!"
— "I have to do it my way!"
Claire doesn't know how
to weave, but she's toiling,
forcing weft through warp
skipping three strands
in her haste to finish.

She must weave this scarf today
before we leave for the *Altenheim*,
Christmas is a far off country
for Claire and Great-Aunt Hilaire,
who waits in a summer gazebo,
and doesn't recall who we are.

I know my mother is hurt —
my child isn't weaving for her
on the loom she herself bestowed
for Claire's seventh birthday.

Claire wets the yarn with her tears:
"I'll never get it right!"

Grandma snorts. "You don't have to
do it if it makes you miserable."

"Oh, no," Claire cries, I'm stopped!"
We grownups watch her snarl a *cul de sac*,
half the threads hanging slack.

"My grandma was the last," says Grandma,
"to spin, but my mother used to weave."
Claire stops crying — Grandma seems to know
how one loop locks another in.

Grandma threads the reeds, telling Claire:
"Pretend the top threads are your mother,
and the bottom threads are me.
You are the shuttle, your only job
is to carry the wool through this shed."

Passing the shuttle to each other,
Together they fold the weft
back and forth upon itself,
and the cloth begins to climb.

Fishing

1.

The plug of thrashing fish
plunged my line deeper,
till I popped it from the water,
shiny black, tail flapping
from my clumsy cane pole.

"A bullhead, watch it!"
Dad yelled too late.
"The barbs stung me!" I cried,
as my finger dripped blood
on my slimy prize.

Matt pulled his hand away
from the ancient creaking jaw
of Grandpa's stuffed Muskie.

As I swam along the outer edge of reeds,
I watched him hook a perch.
He almost dropped his pole
in a lake of dark surprises like leeches.

I hoped no one told my children
the story I heard in my childhood:
A six foot Muskie swallowed a child,
and they only found one foot.

2.

What if now, past seventy
Dad caught another Muskie?
"I've been mean all my life," he says.

But what if the fish were meaner,
and he couldn't haul it in,
or writhing, it capsized his boat?

Grandpa now gives a prize
for the most fish. It's his way
to catch a new generation,
as he hates to go fishing alone.

I was sorry Dad needed to bait
his grandson with a prize.

"Fisherman have to provide
their own bait," says Grandpa,
"and put it on the hook themselves."
Matt recoiled from crawfish.

So he gave up his place in the boat
to his sister who fished with a spinner,
hooking a one pound bass, while Matt
watched on the shore and remembered
we had to leave the lake that afternoon.

When the boat returned at noon, Matt was crying
mad: "You have to give me one more chance!"
"I don't have to *give* you *anything!*"
Grandpa said, "obnoxious kid!" and he spat
in the water, throwing me the line,

I spat back — "Don't call him names!
He wouldn't go because he was afraid."
"I wasn't!" cried Matt, but my father only smiled.

"You shouldn't have ordered your Grandpa around,
but you have to be *smart* to be scared."

I remembered how thrilling the tug
of fish before it broke water,
it could be anything!

I wanted Matt to know
why his grandpa fished,
why he kept going
out a little further every day,
how he always was
afraid and surprised.

Cartographer of Living Maps

Stan unfolded maps with a flourish —
the blue line exploding
into Mississippi,
rushed over the dam's spillway.
We ignored damp clothes,
as Stan explained that puddle clay,
the core of it rolling,
was impervious to churning waters.
In fine spray, rainbows
over the sluice gate,
and our soft gasps.

The rookery swelled with great blue herons,
tornado-blown to Lake Cenaiko's
trees, now studded with nests
where herons huddled over blue eggs,
feather barbs locked against the gusts.
Egrets and horned owls sat too
in brief downy warmth.

Motionless in the stream,
white feathers framing her face,
the great blue heron fished,
darting her beak at fingerlings
to mash them for her fledglings.

Mounting bikes, we followed
our Keeper of Maps, over railroad tracks
into new stands of yellow birch, black ash.
Older trees overtook the trail, oak, maple,
and quaking aspen, opening out to a meadow.
In Elm Creek's limestone pool,

Our children splashed and dove,
while we removed our shoes.

Opening the map, Stan found correspondences —
how way led onto way, stayed within the lines
but beckoned on. He refolded mountains,
caverns, highways and trails, once the kids had seen
beginnings, endings and all routes in between.
In his next map he promised more spidery paths —
ones that could lead anywhere.

In Our Minds' Eyes, the Frozen Lake

Our children's voices took on the chirping
quality of sparrows' liquid song.
Their feet rustled leaves, dislodging
stones that clicked and thudded
on the steep and shifting path.

Stan's muscular legs pushed him up
against the pull of gravity,
while I longed to sleep in the meadow
among lupine and columbine.

Halfway up the rocky foothills
of the grand Tetons I climbed
past exhaustion, hearing the faint notes
of my family in the thinner air —
There they were on ice, grassy hummocks,
and teetering on rocks across the frozen stream.

Young, we parents didn't think of bears
or night falling faster through the sunset
than our feet could walk.
The ranger led us down,
as the moon peered over our shoulders.

Stan said to take pictures in our minds' eyes.
We saw our children in each other's eyes
against forget-me-nots in permafrost.

A resounding whirr rose,
the wind through the canyon
filling the shallows with snow.
An ice-wrinkled blue pool pinged
beneath sparrows' feet.

Frosted branches rubbed together,
a climbing whine that tipped
toward harmony. Pleasing discord
crackled over a glassy meadow's sea.

The Family Procession

The body recedes part by part:
German uncles, their big hearts
lost to bigger bellies — venison sausage, stollen.

The Irish aunts can't draw breath
for all the breaths now trapped by cigarettes.
Aunt Ruth, who once filled biddies' white clay pipes
at wakes, never smokes but she sips.

Middle aged cousins get in line
for the recessional hymn.
We take pictures, though we don't want to know
how much the self goes into hiding.

I'd taped our children's voices
for their great Aunt Hilaire,
and asked for her memories on the other side:
"Thanks for Claire's rhyme and Matthew's story."
As a lady who ignors any lapse in decorum,
she doesn't fill my fifteen minutes with her eighty years.

I can't find a tape of Zurich church bells,
our baby napping in his crib, the open windows
without screens, bells ranged high to low,
in the seed-wafted air.

My brother Tom makes the old ones speak
for his home video. Our parents sit
eating bratwurst by the river.
Resigned, they answer all his questions.
Later Tom discovered he'd replaced their answers
with the bridge to the pavilion.

As Grandma opens her mouth to speak,
Emily, her youngest grandchild,
twirls past the bandstand
and dances on.

Dancing on Water

We hear the first loon
as a rising,
hollow, unearthly scale
soon dwindling
with no resolution.
"Do you worry," I ask my husband,
"about getting old and dying?"

Meanwhile the boom swings — "duck!"
he yells and jibs sharp west,
pointing us toward the inlet,
where mist rolls out behind the female,
which lifts her neck, its white-spotted
patches on black, her necklace.

Rapidly plunging their beaks, they curve
to their plumage. While he polishes his feathers,
she preens, shining her head on her wings.

We, voyeurs, see the loons dance
within the bell jar of their calls.
He intones a tremulous yodel,
her response more moan than wail.

Their privacy grows on air,
as still as a skin of water on a bubble,
enclosing them in the gravity
of mutual attraction.

They ignore our sail boat,
becalmed in the windless
sunset's lull, their spell.

The male loon raises his chest ruff
of whiter feathers until, upright,
he rushes past her.
His webbed feet loop her in.

She scoots by him,
skimming the water, rounding
the seam of her turn.
Her ellipse becomes their figure eight.

They dive beneath our boat —
two sleek beaks and slicked heads
surface, and they resume dipping.
"A ceremony," I say,
but my husband replies, "foreplay."

The female snakes her neck
and turns to glide away
to the lake's wild shore,
where bracken and lightening-bolted fir
give way to bog, its hummocky
peat moss a bed for their mating.

We look though we no longer see,
then the wind returns.
I ask if we should follow them,
but he shakes his head.
"It's not too late," I say.

Withdrawal

in memory of Ethel and Stan

Dying, Great-grandma Marceline
turned her face to the wall,
her back to her daughter, Ethel.
Cussedness, said Stan, is a family trait.

Stan arrived at Ethel's bedside
ten days before she died,
but she didn't greet him.
He was sad but not surprised.

He kept on talking
to her silence and turned back.
She never turned around,
and didn't see his face.
She didn't respond to his hand
on her platinum head.

Stan's own hugs were enthusiastic
until, like a cat, he needed room.
"Leave me be, Henry," he'd say,
a line from the dying hero
in *Red Badge of Courage*.

At Ethel's funeral, face in his hands,
his shoulders shook so hard the pew rocked.

Liminal Moments

A Change in Inner Weather

My husband's wounded white cells
replicate into our future
without his consent or mine.
A slight chilling zephyr
lifts fine hairs on our arms.

How Will We Go On?

After a line by C. Dale Young

When someone with wings cannot fly,
she hitches a ride on the wind.

When someone with feet cannot walk,
he balances on his hands,
then somersaults.

The painter with lovely, futile hands
will let them curl like lotus buds
and use her toes.

Holding a brush
dipped in aloe green,
She'll limn a spruce tree's
mossy bole.

Imprisoned for telling the truth,
a blind man waits
until the dark of a purple moon.

He climbs the wall and leaves
his captors stumbling in the murk,
disabled by light-dependency.

Dependent on you,
the sun I soon will lose,
I watch your coral banner
linger on the darkening sky.

Seeking your warmth,
I pick my barefoot way
through shards on your twilight beach.

For you, I'll be a maverick moon
and shine with candle power
in your night.

Living on the Surface

Diving into the deep *cenote*,
I touched fins with a spelunker
swimming up. The sun-wavy light
on cave walls, banded us with stripes.

Stan handed me a towel — one plunge
was enough, while he sat sun-side.
Living on sufferance of his multiplying cells,
he didn't need to practice for oblivion.

Not for us, the spelunker's tunnels,
narrow passages for portable oxygen
beneath the fragile chalkstone landscape,
the heavy weight of millennia above.

We just visit this water-filled land,
its mysteries so close to the surface,
revealed by ruptures in calcium lace,
a cloud burst, or even an earthquake.

Owning Every Crack of Light

In a downpour, Kimball Street's new river,
following the valley's slope,
invaded our driveway and rushed
over the door's low stoop.
The torrent flooded our first floor's
carpet on concrete, over Mississippi silt.

Stan dug a trench for a drain
that sliced the trees' feeder roots.
The next storm we stayed dry,
forgiven by arborvitae.

Caulking cracks and patching plaster,
we got by with glue and wire,
bucket, pail and mop.

Stan was here long enough
to unlearn worry.
He left the fissured concrete be.
His mortal illness too
could not be fixed.

Our house relaxed with us.
We owned a tolerant place
where we loved and left the rest alone.

The Caretaker Forgets

He rebuffs too much fuss,
so it's dinner on a tray,
basketball, TV remote in hand.

She goes to the opera and forgets him
but going out the door, she
remembers to pirouette
like Loretta Young —
he likes to see her dressed up.

If it weren't for her need to be out
she'd rather stay home with him.
She really would.

A brilliant poem makes her forget him.
Didn't they decide to live
their days one at a time, a normal life,
except it isn't?

An unvoiced truth — dying is lonely.
He says he's okay but he isn't,
so how can she keep forgetting him?

Even in her sleep,
dreams conspire to keep her down
where the rumor of his dying can't reach her.

He tells her he's depressed.
"Will you take an antidepressant?" she asks.
He won't.
He has to do it himself.
Alone.

Our Shadows, Our Light

Last night I wept and was afraid,
wandering from room to room
until I was cold in the attic bed
and couldn't get up again.

I needed to travel to shadows
flickering on the ceiling,
like birds' wings in a barn,
to listen as my breath
settled true
on your breathing.

Now a glass globe swings
to gather in our bed,
rocking slow
prismatic showers on
our counterpane.

The silk of rain so blue —
only caressed skin
is pink and warm.

It's first morning light —
as if you will never die.

Able to Cry at Last

Rivulets sliding down
my cheeks while the mourning
dove mutters and coos.

Salty water seeping
grief, its waters healing.
The dove flies away
when I recall my tasks.

Salt tracks my cheeks,
the corners of my lips, and dries
my tear ducts shut —
Please open!
All I want is to be, just be.

I don't want to exile myself
from the garden and the dove's
soft pleading in the rain.

His Wife

She is jealous of her husband's dying,
this old woman. She envies the vase
of pearly everlasting on his bedside table.
She watches the nurse and thinks,
How dare she touch the body
of the man I love.

His wife is a monster
of selfishness. She hugs their children
but waits for them to leave,
so she can climb into bed with him,
remember the young lovers they were.
Saturday morning, locked door.

She longs to shove his new paramour
out, along with the pain he denies.
His wife's a misery, afraid
he might push *her* away,
all the easier
to thrash in the arms of death.

If only she and he could die
a little death together, she could
go with him part of the way.

Being

"I'm having such wonderful dreams,"
he says, his eyes open.
His last day on earth
is spent being
with us and the spirits.
"Everyone is so kind to me."

Each moment wells for him —
his blood circles slow,
unlike sweat and tears.
The river of his body falls
into a salty, rainbowed pool.

I cry, "Stan, don't go!"
Claire tells him, "It's okay,"
and Matt meets his final gaze.

One Fine Day

for Stan, Edinburgh Castle

We climbed to make our own nests
in the fescue on the hill below the castle.
Men, women and children poked out of heather,
Scots lovage, oval sedge and early hair-grass,
tender as a golf green or a newly seeded grave.

Though cloudberries' amber stained my fingers,
at last, it was One Fine Day when nothing changed.
Dappled in points of light-bearing color,
we could have come from the pointillist's brush,
made eternal — aren't we perfect still?

You broke the spell, my love.
Alone among sun-gilded dozers on the hill,
you cartwheeled to another plush place in the meadow,
moving with winds that rippled the rushes in waves.
You brought us — rolling ever faster — the setting sun.

Just Let the Dark Be Warm

in memory of Stan

A southerner who came North
to be with me and the Aurora Borealis,
he never got used to the cold.
Chills never started with his toes
but invaded his stomach.
I warmed him with my body.

At the end, to conserve
his body's furnace,
an impossible task,
sure to amuse his soul,
I applied hot towels,
to ease his passage as he left.

A Golden Bird Needs to Dance

After Hafiz
For Stan

The eagle's aerial waltz
was far above the feeding rounds
of the robin you once watched.

Your pillow was too deep,
the sheets too heavy
for your fragile frame.
Your ribs were an open cage
for your buoyant spirit.

The robin darted back to his nest,
where needy hatchlings chirped.
Healthy, you fed us well.

Sick, you refused all food
but the thin-crusted pizza
our daughter offered you.

Three small pieces broke
your three day fast.
Pizza, like manna, a gift —
your appetite was love.

You ate for strength
to leave us,
then glided into your dance.

Feasting at the All-Times Buffet

At the Funeral

For friends and relatives

I felt your loving presence
intending our lives to go on.
As if the living flame
of every soul rose
and lead us.

After the Funeral

My tight chest reserves
each breath, until
in my bed in the smallest room,
door closed,
I tell myself *breathe in,*
pause, breathe out —
expanding the walls of my lungs
enough so he can enter, so we
can muse about turning absence
into accomplished love.

Where?

Impatiens leave when they're in the pink
but very tired, as you were. Here for a life
as long as your summers, then gone.

An agnostic who believed, I wandered
the wrap-around deck you built for us,
wondering where you were.

In peace I hoped, after the receiving line
at our front door. Beloved dead crowded our stairs,
you coping with an intimate mingling of souls.
Your mother, once quick with a cuff, was sorry.
Your dad, who left when you needed him,
was more than sorry. Then such joyous forgiveness.

Leaving your photo,
a cheerful display of white teeth,
to greet the rest of the revenants,
you sloped off to your chair.
I heard, "*Hi,*" the I
long in exhalation.

I asked, "Is that you, Stan?"
and "*Hi,*" you repeated
with breathless emphasis.
"Hi darling," I said,
afraid to ask for more.

Ash Wednesday

Once Stan, delighted, crossed
the Mississippi River's source up North —
an effervescing spring —
in five strides.

Years later, as our son carried his ashes,
we couldn't find a New Orleans river bank —
neither steep nor public —
from which to scatter his remains.

Mardi Gras revelers in the Quarter
would soon wear ashes on their foreheads.
In the midst of life, we are in death.
Unshriven, they drank beer.
Laissez le bon temps rouler.
Let the good times roll.

Invited by two priests to be anointed
with ashes, I declined.
I knew we were made of earth
and to earth we would return,
but we had a family burden.

We fulfilled our trust
on the shore of Lake Pontchartrain.
My son let a small wooden craft
slowly sink — releasing Stan's ashes
to the lake, which changed from blue
to gray to green and back to blue.

His ashes moved South,
followed the current to the Rigolets,

a strait connecting Chef Menteur Pass
to Lake Borgone, carried on
Mississippi waters to the Gulf.
We returned him
to the estuary of his birth.

My Poltergeist

As the piano floats up,
I jump to grab a leg but am too late.
The piano bench gently rises beneath me
and I ascend, riding the bench like a pony
until Stan pulls my mount from beneath me.

"This is one prank too far, 'T'-Bon," I say,
which is Cajun French, *Petit Bon*.
"Are you still both short and good?" I ask,
"or wholly mischievous?"

Let our echoes cluster on the ceiling.
I spiral up to hug the wraith I almost see,
but don't. I let myself be held.

New Path to the Garden

a message to Stan

The snow, unceasing
from the azure sky,
is fluff from cotton trees,
descending to the place
you left two falls ago.

Propping up our fences,
I replaced the posts
but kept the shadow box panels —
precise, your design.

Removing forty years of topsoil
for a walkway, his own brick pattern,
our son said to me, "you can't let it go" —
my overgrown beds and garden rooms.
He knew a path would lead me back.

He might have said, back to my life.
Daunted by two years of stinging nettle,
I gingerly dug them out.

We never said goodbye.

You drifted out of your body
like the cotton seeds
as I tried to keep you
in forever-now,
the one with you still in it.

Now I'm on my knees in the loam,
tucking in cleome and cosmos,
self-seeding flowers for next year.

I never wanted next year without you.

I Got the Bone Loss Blues

*...as we age...calcium flows out of our skeletons
into our tissues. — Atul Gawande, M.D.*

Woodpecker who mistakes
aluminum for wood,
my chimney for a tree —
his tattoo wakes me, it takes
turns with the radio's drumming beat,
Art Blakey's, while the pecker's
call is hawked in E-flat,
a one note repetition
that he toots one sharp F higher —
a note I seldom hear, my stirrup
calcified, anvil hammered to my ear.

Ain't no use in *Moanin'* with Art!
Sing it! Sing it! Like Nina Simone —
hear it though you lose the higher tones

or mask the tune in white-thrum
tinnitus, that cranky aspirin side effect,
but still I take that pill
to move my body
to shift my booty,
like Blakey, to the off-beat — weak joint.
It counts, though I curse my knees!

Crazy red-head breaks his beak to get me up,
get out — You lay-abed, it's time
to drill sunflower seed in loam.
Soon up to my aching knuckles
in potash and calcified lime.

I got the bone loss blues,
my poor synovial
articulation, my mineral
sin-syncopation,
migration on the down-
beat,
that calcium pulse off marrow to line
arteries —

I creak and crunch
in my own time.

The Widow Regrets

She has secrets.
And so does he,
even though he's dead.
Call it the subtext of love —
the deliberate kiss,
the thoughtful repair
of a wedding ring.

She thinks he has "passed on"
but doesn't like the phrase.
It sounds like he took a test.
On the other side,
surely he sees
her gray heart.

Oh the ways she failed him!
Does he recognize her feigned sleep now?
The way she hid the money for the cradle?
Will she ever stop grieving the times
he wouldn't let her in?

What should she have asked
to elicit more than "okay"
to the hopeless question,
"How are you?"
Was the answer:
(a) in hell, or
(b) suffering a day on earth?
He didn't deny he was brave.

She didn't make him promise to visit her
or expect his spirit in a cyclone
of whirling dust or a spout of water.

Maybe he had something to do
with the eclipse, the moon
silencing the birds
and blotting out the sun just long enough
for her to burn the book of shame.

Come back, Stan, come back!
All is forgiven. Am I?

Still Here

message to Stan

The invisible tendrils of my life
hold me here to work,
where native purple coneflowers
are eaten by rapacious goldenrod.

Should I give up sprawl
for order and hydrangeas
in my seventh decade,
forgo self-seeders for shrubs,
plants within their bounds?

No — this uneasy balance
between a carpet of violas
and stinging cactus is my destiny,
a way to discover that old hands
can yank the thorn-studded thistle.

Like our marriage,
my garden is still becoming
stronger with its weight of grace.
Just as each floor joist
still bears your presence.

Today, I pull up the spiky devil's rope
and rejoice that instead of just weeding
for the twelve years of your illness,
I tended a fragile loveliness.

The Widow Tries the New Old Age

She startles herself
in the skinny mirror.
Who is this woman
with spiked waxy hair
and retouched skin?
Who cross-hatched her
into the picture?

Where is the serene watercolor,
of a rocking chair,
the photo album open
on her ample lap?

Now everyone expects her
to act like she is only 65,
still young enough to fly
and dance. She ignores her pain.

In five years, when she's eighty,
will she let herself eat cream puffs,
walking old and slow,
like her own grandma?

Something to look forward to,
but meanwhile she has lots to kvetch about.
Busy, busy, busy but first
(no one is looking)
she'll take a nap.

Civic Sadness

Talking to Stan on election day 2016

Acrid smoke from celebratory campfires
follows me home,
where you can't comfort me.
Suspicious of every happy person,
I long for your astringent wit,
your anger.

In the neighborhood, we who are sad
know each other —
by our heavy steps,
halting words,
the way silence drags our faces down.

Where in the Universe Are You?

All the lonely stars
are not you.
On the gleaming table top
is the space you left
and my face alone.

Discomfited by disorder,
I sweep and cry.
Each cold star collects the floating
space debris within its orbit,
scrawled fragments of time.

All the shining, lonesome stars,
once close,
forming a canopy above us,
are far as despair.

Stars do not jig to jazz,
don't smell like parmesan and basil
or slouch in pain,
do not let me kiss your balding pate.
Are not you.

At the Boundary Waters

She can howl if she wants to.
She opens and closes her mouth,
waits for wolves.

The blessed loons moan for her,
fill the weeping dark
with earthy longing.

She keens,
raw throat-scraping cries
no one expects
from a civilized widow.

Approaching the Condition of White

Widows and widowers come to see
the unexpected beauty of the dead.

Wheat celosia's silken pink plumes,
now leached of all color,
transfer seeds to the frozen earth.

Our winters are not hopeless
but stark as the mourning
we must go through.

At the western gate of death,
those who are left
wear white
and carry life.

The Widow Comes to Life

When she was eight years old
she raced in and out of church,
praying quickly on All Soul's Day,
bent on saving many souls
from purgatory.

Now, she hopes to save herself.
She sees purgatory through a hole
in the sheetrock of a puce room
in a nursing home.

She fears a life without man hugs.
She dreams of his unshaven chin,
the way he touched the curve of her hips.
In dreams she relearns the shape of his mouth,
suspecting that spirit and flesh
are one — how else explain the leaping?

Intimacy in Flight

He stands as I brush by him.
We order drinks, his beer, mine chardonnay.
I give him my mixed nuts —
I can tolerate salt on my cheeks
but not on my tongue,
which is weary of the outskirts
of foreign languages.

How long it's been
since a man kissed me on the lips
meaning sex, even love.
We are the only two people
reading — his tome and my detective novel.
As lights dim around us, we continue,
but soon I succumb to light sleep
and lean towards his shoulder,
swaying back before we touch.

Checking In

Wearing leggings again —
unlike the wool-pilled ones
my mother forced
on my stubborn legs —
and a sequined tunic shift,
am I taking a good risk?
Or merely being ridiculous,
an older woman
who needs to wash her mirror?
I can't help asking your advice.

What would you say but "drive carefully,"
as you always said when I left our home
for minor forays into the world.
Tell me, should I shift
my car into second gear
for the snow-packed hill?
When I get there alive,
is it okay to enjoy
someone's hands on my shoulders?
It makes me feel less lonely.

A Solitary Walk With the Spirits

I hear my grandfather's ghost
tap the hollow spiles piercing maples
with his hammer.
Syrup flows
to a five gallon bucket at the base.
Sweetness pools on the snow
like Aunt Maxine's cream candy
setting on marble in Mayville.

A puff-furred fox haunts the woods,
her red coat glistening in the snow.
A cedar waxwing's bandit mask
glints as she preens her coral feathers
and flirts her yellow tail.

A pileated woodpecker rat-a-tats the fir.
No longer tethered by my husband's arm,
I skid on black ice.

Still, I'm sorry for each grain of salt
I tossed upon the ice.
I hear water percolate
the snow, one drop at a time,
until the rivulet seeks gutters,
heading to the river — I know
many ways to slip and fall.

Risk

Sedona

A plunge of blue fills the crevice
in rust-colored rock, and the azure-tinted
saddle curves toward the valley.
I want to spread-eagle myself
upon the central rock, the confluence
of Yin and Yang.

I add one precarious jasper to a cairn
and take hesitant steps on red sandstone.
I fear not feeling the vibration,
as rapidly as before between the poles
of feminine and masculine.

I squat and lower the palm of my hand
close to the vortex in the stony earth
but feel only a quickening pulse
in my thumb, and an absence in the center
of my life line. Slow, I tell my heart.

Scrying the Future

Each day's questions are balloons —
joy would be to set them free,
but they drift back
through cloud-masked starlight.

Will I go or stay?
At night when missing you,
I turn from back to belly
on the dark side of the moon.

Brown ink, crabbed script
fades with its secrets,
drawings of rare orchids.

Big questions strike me dumb.
Answers are heavy.
I'll open my sack of sleep,
unfurl the night's cryptic dream —

You, a gray cat with green eyes,
are purring in your chair.
None of my questions
survive your listening silence.

My Phantom Ring

Winter fell hard on me
after the radiant fall you died.
A pale band of naked skin
circled my cold ring finger
reminding me of the setting sun's
scarlet light on the high snow drifts
outside the church when we married.

Today, sun tanned and empty,
my finger aches, as if just now
I'd tugged my wedding ring off
over the years that made
my knuckle larger.

Time moves through us.
I remember our trembling
contract, you sliding the gold ring
onto my slender hand.
How each small diamond winked alive.

Magic

Before you joined the radiant ones
to live out of time,
I pictured you enjoying simultaneity,
sampling the All-Times Buffet.

You slide into 1967, a phone booth
on Napoleon and Dryads, to wait for me.
Above you, in my antebellum mansion,
in my octagonal room, I'm stylish in high heels.
I draw a thin black line beneath each eye.
Mascara is chic—it's not the night for blue jeans.

You, Stan, are proud to take me to Tre Fontani's
for a five course meal:
Antipasto — chewy bread with artichoke paste,
and olives. You tell me you're in awe
of the universe.
Then *Primo* — spaghetti Marinara,
"Do you believe in God?" I ask, and you say "yes,"
passing our *Secondo* — scaloppini marsala.
"But not a personal God."
You touch my hand.
We inhale the fragrance of a buttery,
wine-suffused roux
then eat in slow motion.

Over *Contorno* — roasted parsnips, potatoes, and leeks,
I explain that the Goddess, Mary,
and Jesus both feel personal to me.
"Why would I believe in a clockwork God?
Or a first engineer?" I ask.
You laugh and kiss my cheek.

Over the *Dolce*, Tiramisu, we agree
that God does not work magic.
You raise your Chianti to toast me,
my 24th birthday.
You tell me you want "someone special"
to spend the rest of your life with.
It's our fourth date, and soon
I break up with you —
I'm too young to be serious.

Your housemate says you're dating
a blonde from Chateau Carré.
Your jaunty back shows you have a life.
I'm jealous and follow you into 1970.

At the Red Lion, everyone laughs at your joke,
but you look at me. "You're funny," I say.
It's raining and you have an umbrella,
which leads to love then marriage,

and a 1971 wedding trip West
where we, two oldest children,
learn to pitch our tent together.

Back in the French Quarter
Over a double order of oysters,
we talk about our families:
yours small, mine large.

You like children,
So you take my hand and transport us
into 1977, where fluorescent lights
hiss at my two-day labor.

With my pain tuned higher
than the wheeling stars above,
out comes Matthew who is magic.

Matt travels in a Swissair hammock
to Zürich, then we three fly back
into 1979, so Claire can be born at home.

Her large eyes meet yours
as you hold her in warm water.
She's proof God's mother loves us.

The Mystery of Dragon Play

We ate and drank beneath a Quetzalcoatl moon.
Our family clan, leaving the occult
mysteries — the temple
of obscure writing in Chichén Itzá —
played in Tulum on a white sand beach.

The cousins recognized the blunt-nosed head
and long tongue when they dug
for the Mayan Vision Serpent.
As its body uncoiled, so did its wings.

Stan and I joined in freeing
the dragon's sinuous length.
Soon its hind legs flexed
to hoist up its great gullet.

Improbable blues ringed the Caribbean
turquoise in the shallows,
royal blue in the mid, gull-flecked distance,
Prussian blue at the horizon.

Like an ancient coin,
a ghost of itself,
the wafer moon rose.
The sudden tropical night
cut the sea from the beach,
and the shore breeze began
pushing against us as we
left the dragon to sleep.

For that one night
our serpent resisted
the tug of the full moon's tide,
the erosion of time.

Your Bright Soul

1.

Gris Gris shot by us, pushing us together,
her matted pelt a blur as she scuttled away.
I, embarrassed, called the dog —
in a low, sexy voice, you said later.
You didn't detect my shy outrage.
I didn't feel like flirting with a man
so vividly handsome — royal blue jacket,
white shirt, your teeth too whitely perfect.

Where I came from, they didn't grow
men so bright in every tingling sense.
If I looked into your dark eyes'
sparkle, I couldn't hear you.
I withdrew when you played Donovan
across Lake Pontchartrain.
You hadn't bored me to sleep,
as you surmised — Far from it.
The abundance of you
took some getting used to.
You won me with your wit, provoking
my belly laughs and sly smiles.

One night you made stuffed artichokes,
filling each leaf with parmesan
and garlicky bread crumbs, a lemon slice
drizzling the mixture as each steamed.

After slowly consuming each leaf,
until only the most tender and succulent
core remained, you didn't rip off
the choke hair to get to the center,
but picked me up instead.

2.

Your illness gave us the gift of now.
We felt lucky to be happy each day
with each other, our old-couple bickering
almost gone. When you felt sad and listless,
shoulders slumped, your body turned
in upon itself, I could only hug you.

The light was muted in your eyes,
until you were loose enough
in your body to spark
with your old scintillation.

When you left, the ceiling grayed
above you, lamps dimmed,
the clock in the kitchen ticked
too loudly, heavy feet on the stairs
came too soon. Through the open door,
I imagined you blissed out
as the brilliant white sky wept.

Your Eyes Possessed the Endless Space

in memory of Stan

Breathless on the Jüngfraujoch's high saddle,
I held our baby in a pouch strapped to my breast.
My eyes were focused on you,
trusting the way you carved a gentle turn
into the mountain's side, the sheer drop-off road.

"Mönch, Eiger, and Jüngfrau," you intoned
relishing the mountain peaks' names in your mouth,
even more than the *spargeln*, white asparagus
with Hollandaise sauce, a spring treat.

As we ate, you followed a sun-blessed eagle,
her wing span wider than you were tall,
who alighted only to feed her young.

Sitting on the top of Europe, you traced rivers
and lakes marking cantons, Bern and Luzern,
and the sun sank into massifs.

Your happiness became mine, a sort of ecstasy
when far stars, one by one, turned on.
Even extinguished fires
marking the death of worlds.

The moon lighted our future faces —
all luminous forever, just as you are.

Old Sol, Old Love

Stems of Lily of the Valley hold
each bell in a spiral, each cup fluted,
hidden in a sleeve of green leaves.
As I bend my head over my work
this spring, I remember you, the way
you crept in stocking feet behind me
to kiss my neck, how I turned beneath
your lips, opening to your warmth.

About the Author

Patricia Barone's latest book, *Your Funny, Funny Face*, Blue Light Press, is her fourth book, third collection of poetry. A previous collection, *The Scent of Water* is from the same press. New Rivers Press published her first book of poetry, *Handmade Paper*, and a novella, *The Wind*. Her poetry and short stories have appeared in anthologies such as *Bless Me Father*, by Plume/Penguin, and *Inspired* by Tagore, Birmingham, England, as well as others from Peter Lang, Prentice Merrill, and Wising Up Press. Periodicals include *The American Poetry Journal*, *The Shop* (Ireland), *Great River Review*, *Pleiades*, *Commonweal*, *The Seattle Review*, *Visions International*, and the *Widener Review*. She has received a Loft-McKnight Award of Distinction in poetry, a Lake Superior Contemporary Writers Award for a short story, and a Minnesota State Arts Board Career Opportunity Grant for a workshop with the Irish poet Eavan Boland.

www.ingramcontent.com/pod-product-compliance
Lightning Source LLC
Chambersburg PA
CBHW020942100426
42741CB00006BA/617